Welcome to Japan

Project Editor Kritika Gupta
Assistant Editors Abi Luscombe, Niharika Prabhakar
US Senior Editor Shannon Beatty
Senior Art Editor Ann Cannings
Project Art Editor Roohi Rais
Assistant Art Editor Bhagyashree Nayak
Jacket Coordinator Issy Walsh
Jacket Designer Dheeraj Arora
DTP Designers Sachin Gupta, Vijay Kandwal
Picture Researcher Rituraj Singh
Senior Producer, Pre-Production Tony Phipps
Senior Producer Ena Matagic
Managing Editors Jonathan Melmoth, Monica Saigal
Managing Art Editor Diane Peyton Jones
Deputy Managing Art Editor Ivy Sengupta
Delhi Team Head Malavika Talukder
Publishing Manager Francesca Young
Creative Directors Helen Senior, Clare Baggaley
Publishing Director Sarah Larter

Reading Consultant Dr. Barbara Marinak

First American Edition, 2020
Published in the United States by DK Publishing
1450 Broadway, Suite 801, New York, New York 10018

Copyright © 2020 Dorling Kindersley Limited
DK, a Division of Penguin Random House LLC
20 21 22 23 24 10 9 8 7 6 5 4 3 2 1
001–316751–Jun/2020

A catalog record for this book is available from the Library of Congress.
ISBN: 978-1-4654-9321-7 (Paperback)
ISBN: 978-1-4654-9322-4 (Hardcover)

DK books are available at special discounts when purchased in bulk for sales promotions,
premiums, fund-raising, or educational use. For details, contact: DK Publishing Special Markets,
1450 Broadway, Suite 801, New York, New York 10018
SpecialSales@dk.com

Printed and bound in China

The publisher would like to thank the following for their kind permission to reproduce their photographs:
(Key: a-above; b-below/bottom; c-center; f-far; l-left; r-right; t-top)

1 Dreamstime.com: Scott Dumas (l); Ziggy Mars (r). **3 Dreamstime.com:** Tashka2000 (tr). **iStockphoto.com:** WinsomeMan
(bc); woolzian (bl, br). **4–5 iStockphoto.com:** f11photo. **5 Dreamstime.com:** Roywylam (t). **6–7 Dreamstime.com:** Sean
Pavone. **8–9 Dreamstime.com:** Jaturun Phuengphuttharak. **9 Dreamstime.com:** Larisa Kurganskaya (ca). **10 Dreamstime.
com:** Vera Aksionava (crb); Ryzhov Sergey (cb). **11 Alamy Stock Photo:** Nic Cleave. **12–13 Getty Images:** imagenavi.
13 Dreamstime.com: Yasuhiro Amano (t). **14 Dreamstime.com:** Sergey Uryadnikov. **15 Alamy Stock Photo:** John Bracegirdle.
16–17 Alamy Stock Photo: Sean Pavone. **18–19 Getty Images:** Charly Triballeau / AFP. **19 Getty Images:** Shoji Fujita (cr).
20–21 Dreamstime.com: Anastasiia Boriagina. **20 Dreamstime.com:** Anastasiia Boriagina (br); Elena Schweitzer (crb);
Jayk67 (bl). **22 Alamy Stock Photo:** Sean Pavone (bl); Chris Willson (clb). **Dreamstime.com:** Hobbitfoot (tl); Sarun Ongvanich
(cl). **Getty Images:** Shoji Fujita / DigitalVision (cla)

Endpaper images: Front: **Getty Images:** Kirsten Boos / EyeEm; Back: **Getty Images:** Kirsten Boos / EyeEm

Cover images: Front: **Dreamstime.com:** F11photo; Back: **Dreamstime.com:** Marian Garai

All other images © Dorling Kindersley
For further information see: www.dkimages.com

A WORLD OF IDEAS:
SEE ALL THERE IS TO KNOW
www.dk.com

Contents

4   Where is Japan?

6   Mount Fuji

8   Cherry blossoms

10   Special clothes

12   Food

14   Snow monkeys

16   Temples

18   Sports

20   Origami

22   Glossary

23   Index

Where is Japan?

Japan is a country in Asia.
The capital city
of Japan is Tokyo.
It is a very big and busy city.

Tokyo

Asia

Japan

Mount Fuji

Mount Fuji is
a mountain.
It is the tallest
mountain in Japan.

A fast train zooms
past Mount Fuji.
It is called a bullet train.

Cherry blossoms

Cherry blossoms are special flowers in Japan. They grow on many trees. The flowers show that Spring is here.

Cherry
blossom
flower

9

Special clothes

These people are wearing kimonos. Kimonos are Japanese robes. People wear kimonos on special days.

Fan

Hair stick

11

Food

Japanese food can be very healthy. Sushi is food made with fish, vegetables, and rice. Ramen is noodle soup.

Sushi

Ramen

Snow monkeys

Snow monkeys live in
the mountains of Japan.
They swim in the
hot springs.

Hot spring

Temples

There are many
temples in Japan.
Some temples have gardens.
The gardens have lots
of flowers and trees.

Sports

Lots of people in
Japan like sumo.
It is a very old sport.
Wrestlers compete
in sumo.

Sumo
wrestler

18

Baseball is also popular.

Baseball player

Origami

Origami is a Japanese art. These are origami shapes. They are made by folding paper.

Glossary

Asia
the biggest continent in the world

baseball
game played by two teams using a bat and ball

hot spring
pool of warm water that is heated by hot rocks

sumo wrestler
someone who competes in a sumo match

temple
building where people go to worship

Index

Asia 4, 5

baseball 19

bullet train
6, 7

cherry blossoms
8–9

hot springs 15

kimonos 10, 11

mountain 6,
7, 15

Mount Fuji 6–7

origami 20–21

ramen 12, 13

snow monkeys
14–15

sumo 18, 19

sushi 12, 13

temples 16–17

Tokyo 4, 5

A LEVEL FOR EVERY READER

This book is a part of an exciting four-level reading series to support children in developing the habit of reading widely for both pleasure and information. Each book is designed to develop a child's reading skills, fluency, grammar awareness, and comprehension in order to build confidence and enjoyment when reading.

> **Ready for a Level 1 (Learning to Read) book**
> A child should:
> - be familiar with most letters and sounds.
> - understand how to blend sounds together to make words.
> - have an awareness of syllables and rhyming sounds.

A valuable and shared reading experience

For many children, learning to read requires much effort, but adult participation can make reading both fun and easier. Here are a few tips on how to use this book with an early reader:

Check out the contents together:
- tell the child the book title and talk about what the book might be about.
- read about the book on the back cover and talk about the contents page to help heighten interest and expectation.
- chat about the pictures on each page.
- discuss new or difficult words.

Support the reader:
- give the book to the young reader to turn the pages.
- if the book seems too hard, support the child by sharing the reading task.

Talk at the end of each page:
- ask questions about the text and the meaning of the words used—this helps develop comprehension skills.

Reading consultant: Dr. Barbara Marinak, Dean and Professor of Education at Mount St. Mary's University, Maryland, USA.